Windows 10:

2021 Beginner's Guide.
Everything You Need to Know
to Get Started with Windows 10.
22 Tips & Tricks Included.

Windows 10

ISBN: 9798706584856

Windows 10

CONTENTS

Windows 10

Windows 10

Windows 10

Introduction

What do you know about Windows 10? Being one of the most popular OSes out there, it's definitely a system that works well, and offers many benefits.

Windows 10

But what can you do with it?

Perhaps you're someone who has been curious about Windows 10, but doesn't know where to begin. Well you're in luck.

In this book, we'll go over what Windows 10 can do for you, and the definitive guide to Windows 10 that you can rely on. By the end of this, you'll be able to use Windows 10 for everything, and who knows, you may learn new things that you didn't know before about Windows 10, helping you better your ability to use it, and help others.

For a lot of people, it seems like a lot, and there are a lot of underutilized functions to Windows 10. But by learning about it, you can use this versatile Windows system to truly master everything, and to benefit you on all fronts.

Windows 10

Chapter 1 – The Windows 10 October 2020 Update

The latest update to Windows 10 happened in October of 2020. It got other updates in the past, but this one does have some great potential to it. In this chapter, we'll go over the updates that this had, why they matter,

Windows 10

and what you need to know about each of these updates as well.

New Edge

Edge hasn't always had the best rap, simply because it's on the same level as previous Microsoft browsers. But, it's since gotten some amazing changes that will definitely impact the system for the better. It is a browser that offers more performance, better privacy, and a whole lot more ease for when you choose to browse. It's fast as well, and there are new features still being added. There is a collections feature added too for content that you find and save online, so if you're doing some research, you can put that all into one place, or looking to get holiday shopping done quickly and effectively, this is one of the best ways to do this. It also works across multiple PCs and devices, so if you want to use this on your devices, then you totally can, and it can be one of the best, most efficient browsers to use for shopping and doing research at any point in time.

Refreshing Beginnings

The start button is a whole lot more refined compared to the way it was before. It also is now partially transparent to the tiles, creating a better, more redesigned app. It also has better app icons, including calendar, calculator, and mail. It also comes with the dark and light themes too, and you can also show the accent color if that's what you're looking for. You can do this for the start, the action center, and the task bar. You do need to go to settings and personalization to do this, but it's pretty easy for you to make it look good, and a whole lot more refreshing as well.

Windows 10

Goodbye System Control

A lot of people weren't really a big fan of the control panel, which was a bit confusing compared to settings. But now, you have the new app for settings that's there. The control panel is now moved over to the settings app, and it does copy everything to there, so if you did have BitLocker settings or other features, that's all there. They're slowly phasing out of the control panel, but a lot of the built-in settings features aren't there anymore, but now a big part of settings, which does in a way make it a little bit more streamlined, especially when trying to find all of the different apps and settings which are out there.

Windows 10

Kick some Apps

You can now access Samsung devices and apps onto your PC.. this is all done from the "Your Phone app, which does have the ability to access your phone there directly. You can now put the android apps directly onto there, and they'll run from the phone, but also you can use them directly with the desktop of Windows 10. With the Note 20 users using this a lot, there is a chance that Microsoft will work with Samsung in order to offer this feature not just to Windows 10, but to other different devices too. The apps that launch in different Windows will also allow you to work with multiple Samsung apps as well. It's the beginning of merging these two major beasts, offering a more streamlined, interesting experience to your device, and to your Windows 10 personalization too.

Windows 10

Easier Pinning

They now make it so that you can make pinned sites a part of your taskbar too. Whenever you pin the site directly to the taskbar using edge, you can now click the task icon to see the pinned browser tabs. So if you want to pin the Gmail account that you use to Edge, and you've got Gmail open in serval tabs, you can click on that icon to look for them, even if they're in other edge Windows. This is good for organization, and is an additional feature that does make Edge a very interesting, and really rewarding system for you too, especially if you're looking to create the best experience possible.

Goodbye Focus Assist

If you're familiar with Focus Assist that hides notifications when you're playing games, you probably remember it being incredibly annoying, and incredibly noisy. Well Microsoft understands that it's very annoying, so you can now have it so that if you do need to look at a notification, there's a summary now. Focus assist will show you now that there is a notification that it won't bother you with that. You can keep this on there, and not keep it on there, and from there, you can of course, turn this off when you're done. You can disable this and re-enable this if you want to use this. So if you weren't a fan of this, this is a great option, and one that can ultimately help make your browsing and use experience a whole lot less annoying, and of course, a whole lot more fun too!

Smoother Advanced Settings

Settings is a great place to look at the device details and other such actions. It also can help with your display settings too. You can simply go to your advance display settings, changing the refresh rate of the display, to offer smoother visuals and better motion, and you can crank this up on gaming PCs too, so if you're looking to have an amazing powerhouse of an experience, this is probably the one setting that you should be looking for, since it's robust, but also offers amazing benefits down the line for you.

Toast Elimination

Those 2-in-1 devices now switch to their different experiences without the notification toast asking you to switch to a tablet mode if you take off the keyboard, or if you change the way the interface is. This may seem like a small and minimal sort of thing, but if you're sick of always being bothered whenever you unplug the keyboard or do just about anything, this is probably one of the best settings to change, since it offers better flow

Windows 10

of your activities, and a whole lot that you can do better too!

X Marks the Spot

If you're one who gets a bit encumbered by the presence of logos and apps, you're not alone. If you're working with a lot, then chances are it becomes overwhelming. However, what you can do now with the new addictions is first and foremost, you will see app logos for every notification that you have, so if you're confused on where it's from, the logo will make it a whole lot easier to work with. There is also the "X marks the spot" feature, so if you want to click on it, look at it, close it, and then go off and do something else, it's all right there, creating a much smoother experience, and one that isn't completely annoying or bothersome either.

Windows 10

Device Management Improvements

This is more for IT professionals or those who use multiple devices, but now there's a device management policy that has new settings for local users and groups that offers more settings that are universal for all of the devices. This is managed directly in the group policy editor, and is a great one to consider as well.

Of course, that isn't to say that it doesn't fix all of the numerous performance and other issues too, since it does offer less crashes and other changes too. The additions that Windows 10 has do span a gamut of different areas, creating the best experience that you can get on a Windows 10 device that you're looking for as well.

Chapter 2 – The Windows 10 Interface

There is a whole lot that goes into Windows 10 and it can be overwhelming, but we'll go over the interface, what it is, and how it helps.

Windows 10

You'll learn by the end of this how to navigate Windows 10 easily, and effectively.

The Start Menu

Our first location is the start menu. This is where you can change your settings, get the files and pictures that you need, or even open up an app or two.

This is easy to open, and you've probably opened this before. You press it, and then go from there.

You can also press the windows key in order to properly open this.

How to Configure the Start Menu

The start menu is very easy for you to organize, change and make additions to, especially if you want to make it your own.

Windows 10

The start menu configuration is good if you have so many apps open that you don't know what to do about it.

This can have specific apps added to it, simply by right-clicking and then choosing to pin that to start. The universal apps however need to be opened up directly from the start menu.

You can also uninstall apps directly from the menu if needed, and it can be good for you to do to help eliminate cutter. To do this, you can click on

Another popular start menu configuration is resizing. This is good if the tiles are too big or too small to look at everything.

In order to fix this, you go to personalization, then start of course, and you can choose the tile size that you want.

Another feature you can also choose here is extra tiles. This is good if you have a ton of apps. Alternatively, there is also an app list, which is good for you to use too.

Windows 10

All of this is done directly by going to the personalization menu, then choosing the start, and you can make it as interesting as you want, which is perfect for if you really want to make it your own, and good for if you want to make it a unique experience for you too.

How to Set the Desktop Background and System Colors

You can set up desktop backgrounds for a fun personalized experience, and it's simple too.

You go to personalization, and from there, you choose the option for backgrounds and colors.

First, let's talk backgrounds. You can choose the background that you want which has a specific theme to it, a premade background.

Alternatively, you can also choose your own. This is gone by going to browse, and you can go to your pictures, downloads, or even create a folder of different backgrounds you want to use.

After you're done with that, you can choose a background color, or whether you want it to be tiled or filled to the screen.

You can also change the colors too, and this includes the menu colors and app colors. To go to this, you choose colors that's underneath backgrounds, and then toggle the one that you want. This is good to do in order to create a personalized Windows 10 experience that you'll enjoy.

The Taskbar

Next to the start button is the task bar.

This is important because it contains pinned applications that you use a lot, along with the notification area.

Windows 10

You can always add different apps by right-clicking them and then pressing the option to pin this to start.

You can also do the same thing by right-clicking these and then choosing to unpin this to start, which is good for those apps you feel are just sitting there taking up space at the bottom of the taskbar.

Task View

Task view is another addition to Windows 10, perfect for those looking for more project efficiency. It lets you jump between different applications that are open, and to help spread these projects onto different desktops. You can get started with this pretty easily too.

To access this, you can press the task-view button, or go to the Windows key and then tab.

You can also right click your taskbar, then

choose to show the task view button for even more ease of use.

This give you a bunch of different tabs that you can look at. With task view, you can also check to see the status of various projects, which is good if you're working on multiple devices and want everything to be uniform.

How to Achieve Multiple Desktops

Multiple desktops is a feature for those who don't have two different machines. It works well with Task View as well, especially for bigger projects.

You right-click your task view to open that up. From there, you look to the right and see a plus sign. Press that.

There you are, you're then given an option for a new desktop. This is of course a virtual desktop, and you can always add more of these too. In fact, you can add hundreds of these if you so desire.

You can also automatically add more desktops by pressing control, windows, and the D key

To switch back and forth between these desktops, you can do this in two ways. First way is going to task view and then using the arrow keys to navigate.

The second option is the windows key, the control key, and the arrow keys all together. This makes navigation simple, and is perfect if you're using many different desktops and want a simple way to navigate through them all.

Tablet Mode

Another feature Windows 10 has is tablet mode. This is good for those who have 2-in-1 laptops, since it offers this feature that makes it simpler.

Windows 10

To turn this on, you go down to the right with the little message option. That's your action center. You then open that, and you'll be given a lot of features to toggle.

Look for the one that says tablet mode, press that, and it will turn off and on tablet mode.

If you tend to brush against your screen and open things up on accident, you can always turn this off, but if you're using your laptop as a tablet, this is an awesome feature to have.

Action Center and How it Replaces the Charms Bar

Anyone remember the Charms bar from windows 8.1? I don't like to remember, but nowadays Windows 10 has a less-annoying variant of this, and it's also a lot prettier.

The action center is good for notifications about apps, including email and social media, and also ways to toggle features of apps.

Windows 10

This includes Airplane Mode, Tablet Mode, Wifi, and even Night Light mode for your device.

This is handy for when you don't feel like trying to change everything directly from the settings menu, or if you just want a quick and dirty way to fix this.

Rotation lock for example keeps your screen orientation all in one place. There is also a Do Not Disturb feature for Windows 10 that's called Quiet Hours, which is great if you're sick of getting notifications.

This action center has it all in one place, and is the perfect alternative to scrolling through different menus.

The Windows Store

The windows store is another area you should get familiar with. That's the bag that's at the bottom of the task bar.

Windows 10

This is where you can download apps, themes, backgrounds, games, you name it. Some of it is free, and some of it does come with a nominal fee, but the Windows Store is great too for downloading updates to popular Windows apps.

Cortana

Cortana is Windows's answer to a virtual assistant that can help with many things.

The goal of Cortana is productivity, and it can help you manage everything from your schedules, calendar, your meetings, and even reminders and alarms.

And just like other smart assistants, it can also tell you facts and information and help with navigating apps.

This personal assistant is good for you to use if you're looking to find something, or you have a busy schedule that requires a lot of time to work on various things.

Universal Office Apps

Finally, let's take the universal office apps.

These are apps that are directly on your device. The video and media player Windows has, your file explorer, your Windows Explorer, and other apps are considered universal apps.

These are automatically on the taskbar when you first boot up Windows 10, but you can always unpin these.

You can't, however, uninstall these since they're automatically on your device. They are useful apps however, and great for making your Windows 10 experience even better.

Some people usually like to tuck these apps away however, simply because it does take up

Windows 10

a bit of room. But if you're using Windows on a gaming PC for example, the Xbox app is great as a universal app, since it's all installed there, and you can access your games easily.

And there you have it, everything that you need to know about the start menu, and how to use this. There's a lot of handy features on there, but they exist for a good reason, and can be helpful with using office.

The menu definitely can be overwhelming for the average user, and some people do get a bit encumbered by the use of this.

Thankfully though, it's pretty easy once you get the hang of it, and we'll also go over some fun tips and features that you can use to make your Windows 10 experience the best that it can be, and one that you can enjoy too.

Chapter 3 – Navigation

There are some important navigation elements to consider, and different things that you should consider when looking at Windows 10. Here, we'll go over the navigation of popular areas, such as the

Windows 10

desktop

The Start Menu

The first thing that you need to understand is that your start menu will be your best friend. This is where all of the applications that you have are. This is something you can customize, and is good if you want to have a full list of everything that you have, and it shows everything which is installed. This includes both the universal apps out there, and those that are downloaded from the app store to your computer.

To find anything, you can simply search it directly in the start menu, or you can choose to open up all of your programs, and from there, you can choose the app that you want. The latter may be tough if you have a lot on there, but it's good for looking for specific files that you have no idea where they are, or apps that you may have installed directly on

Windows 10

the device you have.

File Explorer

This is also really good if you're looking for a more specific document. File explorer is located at the bottom of the task bar, or you can literally just open it directly from the start menu too. This includes all of the documents, pictures and downloads, or even the folders that you have on the device.

This is also really good for you to use if there are documents that you have no idea are included or not. Some people don't like to use this though because it can be a bit hard to really navigate, especially if you don't know where the file is. But if you're saving documents and such to specific locations, or have a specific folder for everything, then you're in luck, because it's all right there.

There are a few ways for you to look for what

you need. You can go to the quick access or resents to help you look for some of the documents that you opened up in the past, and you can from there look for what you're looking for. This is a bit limited though. It does tell you in each document where it was saved, whether directly to the documents on the PC itself, to your drive, or to a cloud storage.

There is also looking through each of the files, which includes your different drives, any external drives such as memory cards or even flash drives, or even on a cloud storage service. This can be good for fully navigating the thing that you need. You also can check different folders too. There is also a pictures folder, which is where all of the pictures you have are directly saved, which is good if you're looking for a picture, but can't find it anywhere in your drives.

Windows 10

The Desktop

The desktop is another way for you to navigate too. The desktop can be where you save certain things. The beauty of saving stuff on your desktop is that if you ever need to go back to it, it's all really just right there. This can make it simple, and effective if you're struggling to find a document, but you have no clue where it might've ended up.

The one limitation to the desktop, however, is the cluttered nature of it. If you're trying to navigate a desktop with a bunch of documents, files, folders and apps on it, it can be very cumbersome, and for some people, it can be a bit overwhelming. But when you do find what you're looking for, you can left-click it to run it or open it, or right-click that in order to open it up and look at the properties of this, which may be helpful if you're looking to customize certain parts of this.

Another option to this though for navigation,

Windows 10

is virtual desktops. This is good if you want to have certain desktops for organizing everything. In order to add this, you can press task view directly on your taskbar, and then, you can press in the right corner that plus sign that says new desktop. You can always go to this and delete it whenever, but this is really good if you're working on a bunch of projects and apps and don't want to have them all cluttered into one place.

Navigation of the Windows 10 desktop can be a bit complex at times, but once you get the hang of it, it's pretty easy, and there is a whole lot that you can do with it.

Opening and Closing Windows

Every time you open up a new folder or program, you will have it all out there, and it will be there. There are a few ways to make this go away if you don't want to see it, or if you're looking to make it bigger.

on the very left of a window, you will see the option to minimize this. It essentially will hide it from view, putting it in the taskbar, and you can always click on that icon to show it up again. There is also the maximize button next to it, which literally does the opposite and makes it fit the whole screen, good for if you're reading documents or any such thing on your device.

Then there is the restore button. You will notice that when you maximize the screen, there is a button that shows up called the restore button. If that appears, you can click that, and then return that to the size that it was before. Finally, you've got the close button, which is used to close your window, and delete it from the taskbar if it's the last window that's a part of this.

You can always move Windows too if that's what you want to do. To do this easily, you can simply grab the window that's right there directly in the middle, moving it around. You can always resize it too by moving it to the

Windows 10

corner, where it will automatically resize.

And there you have it, everything that's important about changing, resizing, and navigating Windows for any documents and files that you may have, to make it easier for you to really get the most out of your Windows 10 experience, and to make it the best that it can be for you!

Chapter 4 – Top 10 Windows Apps

There are plenty of Windows apps, but not all of them are created equal. Here are the top 10 Windows apps for you to choose from, and we'll go over why they are good, and some of the other factors that go into these Windows apps for you to use.

Affinity Photo

This is a great one for those who would like to get into photo editing and manipulation. If you're passionate about this, it may be good. This is also a great way to use an alternative to Adobe Photoshop that works well for functionality, and you're not paying a pricey description with this one either. Affinity photo is also a pretty simple one to learn too, which is good if you're starting out. You can also install this on all of the machines that you have. it is similar to Photoshop, but without the hefty price increase that photoshop gets from time to time, and there are still new features being added regularly, so it's a good thing for you to use if you're looking for simple, yet effective photoshop skills to learn.

Windows 10

Ninite

This is a great option for desktop applications. To use this, you choose the desktop applications that you want to put on there, and it will download the latest version for you. It supports over 90 different programs, and you can use this for multiple machines. If you're running company computers that need specific software on them, then Ninite is good for you, since it helps not only download this quickly and effectively, but also offers the best system for you to use, and one that offers a lot of extra benefits too!

LastPass

This is a great one to help you track your passwords. While it is hard to keep track of passwords, this is a great one because it helps not only save passwords, but also adds the ID and the passwords to other apps too, and it even can offer different combinations for you to keep other people guessing. You can simply try out what you want to use, and if you're not a fan of Last Pass, there is 1Password which is also a great option. If you're someone who forgets their passwords like crazy, this is a valid option, and a good one to consider too.

Treesize

This is a good one if you're someone who runs out of space, and it can be good if you're not sure whether or not you have something taking up space too. It stinks when you're running a device only to find out that there is something taking up a bunch of space. It may tell you things that you already know, such as maybe most of your drive space is due to photos, but usually it will tell you the files that are really eating up space. There is a free app, but also a premium one, which is good if you want a more in-depth look at what the heck is eating up your space.

Malwarebytes

If you're someone that is worried about malware, and doesn't have any clue on whether or not you have some on your device, this can be good for you. It's a really good one to have, so you don't have to worry about your files being screwed up. You can run this, and eliminate any of the malware that's sitting there. This is one of the best anti-malware options out there, since not only is it good for cleaning up, but it can also detect other problems for you. There is also a version that's free too, which is perfect for people who are looking to have a quick cleanup of the malware on your device.

Windows 10

WuShowHide

This is really good for any bad patches and issues. If you notice that you're having issues due to an update, or if there is an update that's known to be a problem, you can use WuShowHide in order to hide those updates or even block them or prevent them from being installed, which can be good since some of the updates that are a bit finnicky at best, and at worst, malicious software which isn't good for your PC.

File History

This is a great one that is actually free for users of Windows 10. This will automatically create a backup file for your device. Once this is enabled, you'll have automatic snapshots made of your files, so if you need to go back to a previous version, with a simple right click, you can do so. It's also good to help in the event that something doesn't get backed up, since it can of course, prevent the chance that there may be problems down the line, and issues with attaining different files which may be there. It also helps if you have a specific version that you need, and something that'll help keep everything all in one place.

Recuva

This is a way to bring up some of the deleted files that you have. did you know that when the recycle bin is emptied, the files aren't necessarily destroyed, but instead, the space that they were in now has new data. If you do delete files on an SD card or a USB drive, it's the same way, but the recycle bin is more of a safeguard. Recuva can help get these bag. You can use one of these free as a personal use, but if you plan to use this for multiple

Windows 10

licenses there is a premium fee charged. It can undelete this data and bring it back. So if you accidentally deleted something or haven't added any new data, this can work. This is good if you do accidentally press the delete key too fast, or if you end up losing some deleted stuff.

Speccy

This is a way to look at the inner parts of your PC, and is a valuable app to make sure that everything is working well on your Windows 10 machine. It offers a SMART report for the drive directly, with a report for the US itself that includes the antiviruses that are being used, any updates that are needed, tasks which are scheduled, different frameworks installed, and other such reports. This is good because it can help you make sure that you are running the proper software, and, if something does go amiss, this is a chance for

Windows 10

you to make sure that you can fix it and replace it as needed. They're both made by CCleaner which also is a good way to clean out the software, and this is a good way to make sure that the diagnostics of your PC are in proper order and kept in the proper state.

Wox

If you're familiar with Alfred on Mac, this is very similar. It's a free software of course, and it brings a launcher that's similar to Mac that helps you find the files and apps that you're looking for, or it can help you quickly search the web. If there is a lot of files that are on your device that clutter the system, and you're struggling to find the right ones, this is a good way for you to use it. It also offers different plugins to help with proper searching, and it can even translate languages directly within your launcher too, in order to make it the most effective, useful apps for you to search for things. While the Windows 10 start menu is decent for searching, if there is something very specific or language-focused that you want to look into, sometimes that's limited, and it can be a bit cumbersome to look for this. Luckily, with this app, it offers a more in-depth look at what exactly you're looking for, and some of the other aspects that can help you properly find and get the items that you need.

With all of these apps, there's a lot that goes into this, and a lot of people definitely can benefit from these apps. They're good not just for running your PC properly, but also, to help you make sure that you get the most that you can out of this, and other important tidbits that can markedly benefit your experience too.

Chapter 5 – Tips and Tricks for Everyone

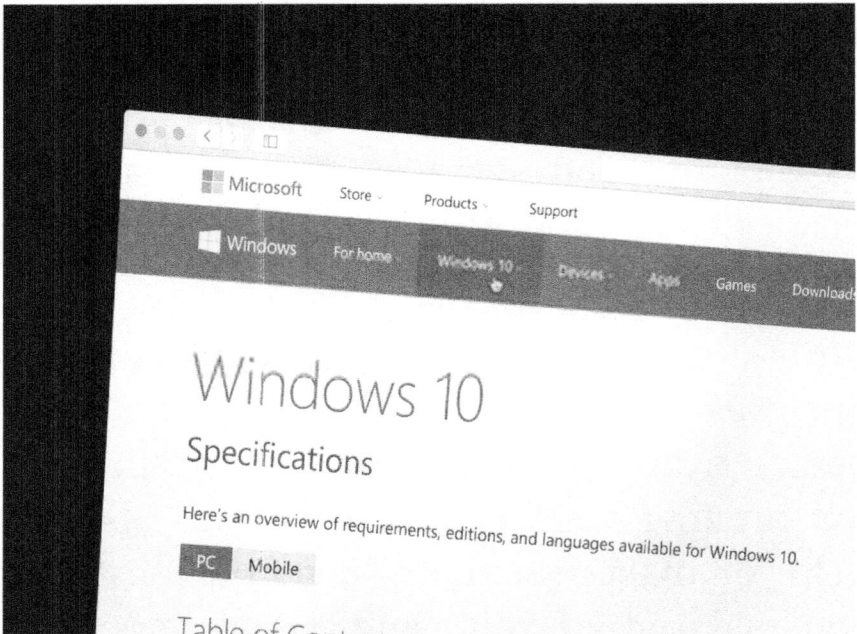

Here is a wide list of different tricks that are important for your Windows 10 device, and we'll go over what they are, and how to do them as well.

Windows 10

Adapting the procedures for your Environment

The PATH can be changed directly on Windows 10, which is useful for changing the environment that you have on the device.

This also includes settings and other variables.

To begin, you need to go Start, and then type in "env" and open up the choice to change the system variables.

You're then given an option on what you want to do with the environment, either create a new one, edit it, or even delete it. You can also dismiss this too.

You may, if you change variables for apps, have to restart them before they go into effect. You can also check the PATH by going to PowerShell and then going to what is called the $env:PATH in order to check and see if the environment that's there is working rightfully.

God Mode

This admin tool lets you change the programs that you have, the network the computer is on and the connections, and many different system settings. For those who use their computer for programming or other activities, this is useful.

It used to be hidden, but now is a feature that's easy for you to find. To use this, you need a folder which is blank, and then you must give it a name. you right-click the folder on there, then go to the option for new.

You then want to choose the new folder that you have, and once there, you press F2, change the name, and of course, change any administrator or system settings that'll pertain to using this. You can also change the credentials and logins as well.

Cloud Clipboard

The cloud clipboard is an enjoyable feature if you're working not just with Windows 10, but other Microsoft devices.

Everything that you write on there is automatically copied to the devices with the same accounts. So if you're working on a project for school and have the essay in cloud clipboard, it can be accessed from another PC or even a mobile phone.

To start this, it requires a manual switch. You need to find cloud clipboard in settings to turn this one on, and you'll then be given the option to choose the devices that you want to use this. This is handy for those specific devices that you plan to use.

You can only use this with windows accounts associated with the clipboard. .

Windows 10

Timeline

Task View, or Timeline, is another handy feature.

This shows all of the activity on this device, and what's happening on your other devices too. This, along with cloud clipboard helps you if you're doing different projects, so you can continue where you finished.

You can use this with both computers and mobile devices, so long that it's signed in. Task View is located right by Cortana to the right.

There's a small little box when you see this. You can then press the right-click to go to task view, and then to timeline. You can also press windows and tab together to get to this automatically too. It will have everything associated with that account there, so if you're looking for something specific, it's all

Windows 10

neat and handy, right there. Great if you're looking for project files, or anything on another windows account.

Sticky notes on Windows 10

Sticky notes is another handy Windows 10 feature. This is great for those who are note takers and use Windows 10.

To go to this, you go to start, and then sticky notes.

All of your notes will be left there, and you can see all of them by double-clicking or tapping them to open and close.

This is also useful because it can be used on default apps too that work with Windows 10.

You can go back and forth with this in order to effectively check different notes that you have on your device.

Windows 10

Privacy Settings

We'll mention this in the next chapter, but privacy settings are incredibly important for Windows 10.

This is because locations, privacy reports, and error reports are automatically sent if this aren't checked off. This can be a privacy concern.

Make sure you take time and check the camera settings, location settings, and reports settings to prevent tracking by Microsoft, and make sure with every new computer you get, you look at these.

This is something oftentimes disregarded by new users, but it's very important to make sure the privacy settings are turned on the way you want, so your information is kept safe.

Windows 10

Game Mode

If you're using Xbox or gaming on Windows, there is a game mode on this.

This turns your computer's settings up so you're getting the best gaming experience.

However, it does eat up a ton of battery, so if you're not using the laptop to game, you should turn this off. You can do so by going to settings, choosing game mode, and then turning that off.

This does allow for more battery life, but if you do go back and forth between gaming and other uses for the laptop, make sure to turn this on once you're done if you're playing a game.

Scrolling inactive Windows

One neat feature that Windows 10 added was

the shaking inactive windows feature.

To enable this, you simply hover the mouse right over this so you can scroll down different tabs that you're reading without having this taking over your whole screen.

To activate this setting, you go to settings, devices, choose the mouse and touchpad option, and then look for the option to scroll these windows.

It isn't automatically turned on, but it's a good feature if you want to read something without it hogging the whole screen.

Shake to Minimize Windows

If you remember Aero Shake from Windows 7, this is the same thing. You click on the tab to open this, and then literally shake your computer horizontally.

This will close everything minus the one that

you're currently looking at. Good if you have like fifty tabs open and you don't feel like closing all of them, so it's done in one fell swoop.

Sharing files with Nearby Devices

You can automatically share files to nearby devices.

This does require the Edge browser to be used, so make sure you're using that first and foremost.

Next, you want to go to your action center, and then look for the option that offers nearby sharing. Toggle that on, and then do that with the PC or phone that you're using.

From there, you can share different files that you have from file explorer, and you can then right-click, choose to share that, and then send it to the other device.

Windows 10

On the other one, you can choose to either open it or save it when it shows up.

The same goes for links. You go to settings, choose the file to share, and then the devices that'll receive this, so you can open this in the other window when it ends up there.

Customize the Lock Screen

You can customize the lock screen in a couple ways.

First, you can go to settings, your personalization, and then the lock screen.

From there, you can choose the different types of lock screen settings that you want, including moving lock screens, lock screens with different pictures to show, or even an image that's tiled or fitted to the screen itself.

Windows 10

Display an image as the Lock Screen

The easiest way for you to change your lock screen is to show a specific image.

This is simple to do. First, you choose settings, personalization, and then you want to look for the option for lock screen.

From there, you can choose the lock screen image you want, and you can choose the background that you'd like for this, or any other options.

From there, when choosing a specific image, you can go to your drive and pick a file that best fits what you want.

Displaying a Sideshow of Images as Lock Screen

Another common way is to show a sideshow of your lock screen.

Windows 10

You go to the same place as you did for choosing an image, and from there, you choose instead the slideshows option.

This takes you to different pictures and files on your computer, including moving pictures and still ones. You can choose the ones that you want, and remove ones that you don't want before you add them.

The easiest way to compile this is to make a folder, choose the images you want, and move them to that folder. When it asks for the images you want to use in the slideshow, you choose that folder.

There are also advanced features too that are done by going down. This gives you the option for camera roll, from your PC, and for ones that fit a certain resolution.

You can choose ones that are from a specific folder, and the ones that only fit the PC. This offers numerous custom options, especially if you're looking to add specific images to this.

Windows 10

Display the Windows Spotlight Lock Screen

There is also the Windows Spotlight option for your lock screen. This uses images that Bing brings up that have some interesting facts to them sometimes. These can be new images every single time.

You go to that same lock screen area, and then you can choose the option for windows spotlight. This is neat especially if you're not particular about certain images, and also want something aesthetically-pleasing.

Display Tips on Lock Screen

You can also show off the display tips too. These can get annoying though.

To turn these on, you go back to advanced features in the lock screen area, and toggle on whether you want to display tips or not.

Windows 10

Some people prefer to turn this one off since it looks much cleaner and a whole lot more professional than to have it on and clogging the screen.

Display App Status information in Lock Screen

Some people like to show the app status in the lock screen. This is really good if you want to see the status on an app, or new notifications.

You can add this by going to the lock screen area once again, and then in advanced features, you look for the option to have apps show statuses, you can press that plus sign, and then choose the app you want to see more of. If there aren't any chosen, you won't see any features.

You can also look at the quick status by choosing apps to show this, but again if you choose none, nothing will appear, so make sure you choose something before enabling.

.

Apply and Manage Themes

Another fun thing is themes.

Themes are good not just for lock screens and backgrounds, but it's next level personalization.

There are some preset themes in the Windows 10 settings already. You want to choose personalization once again, and then choose themes. You're then given different themes to check out, and this includes premade ones, or ones downloaded or created too.

This is fun, and can offer a super personalized and amazing experience.

Windows 10

Display the Installed Themes

If you choose to go with a premade theme, it's very easy. You want to first go back to the theme are in personalization.

From there, you can press the choose theme, and you're then given as bunch of themes that Windows 10 has automatically. You can choose them to load it as a test image, and from there, you can choose which one you want.

If you find one you like, click that, then close it, and then there you go.

To Apply an Installed Theme

Applying a theme is very easy. You can choose a theme that you want, and then press that apply button.

This applies that theme automatically, and

you can install and use it if that's what you feel works for your device.

Installed themes are good to start with, especially if you like different themes, but want to try it out first before adding it.

To Save a Custom Theme

Some people like to go the extra mile and do custom themes. These are good if there's something specific that you want.

To choose a custom theme, you simply go back to the themes area, and then press that option for custom themes.

This is where the fun begins. You can choose the images you want to use as your lock screens, wall papers, and whatnot, or even what pictures you want as a fun slideshow.

Your colors also change here, and you can toggle the colors and fills for this to in order to make it look unique.

You can also choose light and dark mode themes too, which is good to help reduce eye strain as well in most people.

There is also a great transparency effect which can help if you have certain themes which won't work otherwise.

You can even change your mouse curser to make it something fun and unique, and what sounds are made when you click on things. This does get a bit much at times, but you can always change it back if you dislike something.

After you've done this, you simply save the theme, name the theme that you have, and then apply it. There you go.

If you're not a fan of the themes that they give you, or just want something a little bit different, then you're in luck. This is a great way to get started with it, and a good way to use themes that you enjoy.

Windows 10

To apply a theme from the Store

You can also apply themes directly from the Microsoft store, or even online.

Be forewarned if you do the latter, you should be careful so that there aren't any viruses and whatnot on this. This however is rare to happen.

To get themes directly from the store, you simply open up the windows store, find themes, look through, and then download it.

From there, when you're choosing themes, you're then given different ones that you'll like to use, and it'll help offer a truly unique experience for your device too.

To Remove a Theme

Sometimes you're tired of a theme, but that means you can fix it!

Windows 10

To remove a theme in Windows 10, you can simply open up those settings once again, then choose the personalization option, and then, right click the theme you'd like to remove.

Then, press the option to delete it. It's that simple, and pretty easy for you to do.

These are some of the many tips and tricks that come with Windows 10, and are great to use in order to enhance the experience, and make it more fun than ever before!

Chapter 6 – Troubleshooting

Sometimes things don't work perfectly with Windows 10. Here are some ways to troubleshoot Windows 10, including some of

Windows 10

the more common issues that go into this, the tips that go into this, and what you can do with it.

The "Fix it" Tool

While Windows 10 is a much more stabilized system than it was say a few years ago, it still can have some small issues that can affect things as well, and using the fix it tool can help you identify the various issues that surround it quickly and effectively to make it the best that it can be. (ow)

This fix it tool offers different troubleshooters to help with solving the problems that you have with the PC. To run this, you need to go to start, then settings, then update and security, and then, it will give you the troubleshoot feature, and you can also choose the find troubleshooters at the end of the page to help you start. You can choose the troubleshooter that you have, such as internet issues, your updates, and audio issues, and from there, once you choose that, you can then choose to run your troubleshooter.

From there, you can let the troubleshooter continue to run, and then, if there are questions, you can answer them. If you do see a message that there are no changes or updates needed, you can look into the recovery options, and then look at the error codes that come with this too. This is good if you're having issues, but don't know the exact location of their occurrence, and sometimes, the issues may be resolved with a simple Windows update too.

Upgrading Issues

There are some that struggle to upgrade from previous windows systems to current windows systems. There are a few things that you can do.

Windows 10

The first, is to check your settings and see if it requires an update. Update that, and then from there you can download Windows 10 and put it on there to make it work. It can work for older and new devices.

You can also disable what's called Execution Prevention to help with settings. This is done by going to bios, and if that is turned on you can turn this off. Then restart it, and see if it works once again. This may solve all your issues with Windows 10

Removing Forced Updates

Forced updates are annoyingly common with Windows 10. This was something that older windows relied on, but if you don't like that, you can always turn that off. You can go to the Group Policy editor in order to do this. To there, you will want to enable something that tells you when updates are, and will provide notifications. This of course will give you notifications every time this updates.

This may still be annoying for some, but it is an option for those looking to use Windows 10, but don't want to have the automatic restart, which causes precious and valuable time and work to be lost. These notifications however will still show up in your Windows Defender to remind you even when disabled.

Storage issues After Updates

Some people don't know that even when you update Windows 10, the old Windows 10 is still on the device. This is named Windows.old in your drive. It's located in the C drive, and it takes up a ton of space.

To get rid of this, you can go to the cleanup, look for the installation used previously, and you can look for this file.

This normally takes up a lot of drive space, but once you find it and delete it, it should free it up. It may also be buried, so using a cleaner or other software that helps you find files is recommended.

Turning off Notifications that Aren't Necessary

Notifications are a necessary evil for Windows 10. You need them to keep up to date on important stuff, but sometimes...they're very unnecessary.

Notification clogging is very common, but you can turn this off in settings by choosing notifications, and then there's little tabs that tell you what give you notifications and what won't.

Toggle as needed, but it's recommended that you keep notifications for software updates on to be in the know on what's going on.

Windows 10

Fix Privacy Settings

Windows 10 suffers from major privacy issues, from the first edition to even the October update. Sometimes as well, when you update, these get turned on again.

You should update these a lot, and review them as needed. You can go to settings and privacy, where you're given various options on what to turn on and off.

It's recommended to turn off the following:

- Mic and camera
- Location settings if not needed
- Microsoft sending you advertisements
- Using your data for advertising
- Automatic sending of diagnostic reports to Windows

A lot of people worry about their privacy being compromised with Windows 10, and while this was a much larger issue when it first came out, this is still a major focal point.

On that same note, there is the Inking and

Windows 10

Typing section that has a lot of privacy breaches you should fix. This includes what keying you do on this device, so you should make sure that if you do have these on, you take some time to look for them.

You also can control whether you want the cloud to upload your documents. Some people do like cloud storage since it does offer space for all of your documents in one place, but some worry about the security issues associated with this.

Finally, you should go through and disable something called wifi sense. While this does help you automatically connect to different networks, this can compromise data especially with shared networks and public hotspots. If you have sensitive information, turn that off.

Finally, disable wifi services too. These are paid services, but do involve taking information to advertise to you, and if you don't want Microsoft using that advertising data, this should be shut off.

Windows 10

Privacy settings on Windows 10 are very easy to change, but the problem with them is that most people don't realize they exist until down the road. Get in the know on this early on, so you can protect your computer and the data that you have on it especially if it is sensitive information.

Safe Mode

Finally, you may need safe mode. This is used to help with diagnostics, especially if your computer is struggling. If you're in trouble in a Windows sense, Safe Mode is probably your best friend, and it's annoying because F8 isn't the way that you do this. To access it, you need to restart, holding the shift key on the left hand side, or you have to go into update and security, and it can be a struggle. There is also the option of a boot time option for safe mode that you can put together, and from there, you'll have a backup in case you

Windows 10

do get in a jam. You an highlight this option when booting, so that you can boot directly into safe mode as needed too.

For a lot of people, Windows 10 is a simple, yet effective system for them to use in different ways. But it's not perfect, which is why, if you do struggle, you can always try these different options, and see for yourself what you can do to make your experience not only easier for you if you're struggling to understand Windows 10, but also to have the best security possible if you know that your computer may be compromised as well.

Windows 10

Conclusion

Windows 10 is a great system for those who are looking for one that they can use to create a fun, really personalized experience. It's the most personalized Windows experience that you can have, and one that you can create and really enjoy too.

Windows 10

With that being said, if you're not using Windows 10 yet, you should definitely take a moment to look into this. Downloading it is easier than it's ever been, and there are ways for you to download it fully as a media creation tool, and also directly from the site as well.

When you're done with that, you can from there create your best Windows experience that you can, and also download some apps that you can enjoy, and ones that you will love.

From there, you should use the Windows 10 system as much as you can. Get familiar with it, and try to use virtual desktops and other such elements. With the advent of Windows 10 being one of the best OSes for a variety of reasons, for how easy it is, to the customization options, it's good for a lot of people, and if you do eventually want to get the business or education versions, they are available, but usually people just need the home to start with.

Windows 10

Windows 10 has a lot of neat features, and you can use this to your advantage, with this guide as a helpful tool!

Windows 10

I hope, that you really enjoyed reading my book.

Thanks for buying the book anyway!

Printed in Great Britain
by Amazon